SECRETS OF A FORTNITE FAN

MORTIMER

KU-012-619

Published in 2021 by Mortimer Children's Books Limited,
part of Welbeck Publishing Group Limited
20 Mortimer Street, London W1T 3JW
Text and illustration © Welbeck Children's Limited,
part of Welbeck Publishing Group Limited
ISBN: 978 1 83935 045 0

Writer: Eddie Robson
Illustrator: Oscar Herrero
Designer: Dani Lurie
Design Manager: Matt Drew
Editorial Manager: Joff Brown
Production: Rachel Burgess

A catalogue record for this book is available from the British Library.

Printed in the UK
10 9 8 7 6 5 4 3 2 1

All game information correct as of November 2020

SECRETS
OF A
FORTNITE FAN

EDDIE ROBSON

CHAPTER 1

So it's Tuesday lunchtime and I walk into the playground to see what my mates are doing.

But as I go over to them, I catch a bit of what they're saying and I think, Uh-oh.

They're always talking about Fortnite these days.

'...and I found an epic shotgun on the ground right after landing,' Leon's saying as I walk over, 'and I took out three guys in the same building. One was a John Wick.'

Ellie doesn't believe him. 'You never get an epic shotgun just lying on the ground.'

'I dunno,' says Sana, 'a couple of seasons ago -'

Jake interrupts her. 'You never get one. He's making it up.'

Leon shrugs: 'I'm just good at finding the best loot.'

'It's all luck,' mutters Ellie.

And they go on and on like that. Blah blah blah.

You see how I'm not talking?

That's because I've got nothing to say. Because... I've never actually played Fortnite.

Yeah, I know, I know – but when Fortnite came out I was more into Minecraft and Roblox and I never got around to it. And now... I'm sort of... scared to have a go at Fortnite. Because everyone else is really good now, and I don't want to be a useless noob.

I'm not gonna tell them though, because if I'm rubbish at it they'll make fun of me, which is even worse than just standing here while they ignore me and talk about Fortnite.

ME: Tyler Meeks, complete Fortnite noob.

But I want to be able to, you know, talk to my friends. So I'm gonna try it. Today.

SANA: Doesn't need to boast

LEON: Thinks he's a Fortnite master

ELLIE: Won't let you get away with anything

JAKE: Wind-up merchant

What most people talk about when they talk about Fortnite isn't actually what Fortnite originally was. OK, here's what I mean...

The original Fortnite was a game where you got together with other players to build a tower and defend it from zombies.

But the people who made it came up with a Battle Royale mode set in the same world.

(The name 'Battle Royale' comes from a Japanese film which Mum and Dad have, but it's on the shelf where they put things that I'm not supposed to watch yet.)

Basically, a hundred players are dropped onto an island and fight, and the last one standing wins. It's kind of like the Hunger Games if you've heard of that. And then Fortnite: Battle Royale became way more popular than the main game!

When I get back from school my best mate Alfie comes round. He's never played Fortnite either, 'cos his parents don't approve of games with violence and death and stuff. He pretends he just isn't interested in Fortnite, because that's less embarrassing than your parents banning you from playing. But I think he's going to be interested to see me play it.

I've pointed out to him that he could just play it when he's here and no-one would know. But he doesn't want to, because he's not very good at lying, especially to his mum and dad.

ALFIE: lives over the road. Goes to a different school. Idiot.

There are different modes in Battle Royale - you can play Solo (just you against everyone else), Duos (you and one other player working as a team) or Squads (four players working as a team). I'm doing Squads because I need all the help I can get.

How hard can it be? Huh. Turns out, it's pretty hard.

So this is my ninth attempt.

'You lasted four seconds after hitting the ground that time,' Alfie says.

I tell him I know.

'That's your best effort yet,' he says, all cheerful. 'Well done, mate!'

This is getting ridiculous. I'm about to give up. No point, I'm useless. Then a message pings up on my phone.

you took the fortnite plunge then?

Right. I forgot Sana is in my friends list and can see what I'm playing.

Wait, was she in any of those matches I just played? Did she see me? Hope not. That'd be really embarrassing.

that was me who got you with that grenade a couple of matches ago. sorry. i'm swiftshot09

Great.

wanna come to the battle lab?

I ask Alfie if he knows what the Battle Lab is. He doesn't. But then an invite flashes up on the screen - so I go into Battle Lab, skydive down...

And there she is, **SwiftShot09**.

SANA IN FORTNITE

'She looks much cooler than you,' Alfie says.

'That's because she is,' I tell him. Then I look around - seems like we're just on the normal island. 'So what do I do here?'

I have a walk around, thinking it's nice to see the game world without having to worry about other players... and then I fall off a cliff and die.

But in Battle Lab you respawn immediately - so a few seconds later I'm skydiving again, and I hit the ground.

Sana's collected some good loot, and she shares it with me. She suggests I practise using the different weapons. I lob a grenade into a nearby building and blow the place up.

I'm having fun now!

Lots of players never bother with the Battle Lab but it's really handy. You can play a session with friends and do your own private match, with different settings - like a mode where the only weapons are sniper rifles, or where everyone only has 1% health so the smallest hit will take them out.

Or you can use Battle Lab for practice, like I'm doing.

You can wander around the map and see what's where - the storm only closes in after four hours so there's lots of time to try out different weapons.

It's also perfect for practising your building - all harvested materials drop ten times what they usually do in the game.

Even if you're good at Fortnite, the Battle Lab can still be a good place to go if you want to try something new before you do it in the game - like if a new weapon's been introduced and you don't know what it does yet!

When I get out of the Battle Lab, I gear up to go for another round. I know what I'm doing now. Alfie says he's sure that this time I'm going to slay it, or at least, rank higher than #93, and then he goes to the kitchen to get himself a Coke Zero.

While I'm waiting in the lobby, I get some more texts from Sana...

stay on the battle bus until the end!

seriously this is the best tip i can give you. I know it's boring watching the bus fly over but it's worth it. try it

Okay...

oh and don't forget to thank the driver

I didn't think it mattered where I jumped out, really. I've just been bailing out right away. So while the other players dive out, I hang back, wondering why Sana told me to do this. Maybe something really cool happens?

...no, nothing cool happens. You just get kicked off the bus when the time's up. So what was the point of that?

I dive down to the ground and I'm like *quick quick get a weapon, any weapon will do, just grab something before someone shoots you* –

And that's when I realise. Nobody's shooting at me.

Every other match I've played, there've been loads of other players around, scrapping over loot.

Er... where is everyone?

The big building I landed next to seems to be empty, so I search it from top to bottom.

Pretty soon I've got more loot than I can carry.

In fact I'm getting stressed out because I've found a tactical shotgun and I don't know if I should drop something else so I can pick it up.

'Wow,' says Alfie, walking back into the room. 'You're not dead yet! This is incredible!'

'Yeah,' I say. I'm thrilled. I feel powerful. 'So, er... what do I do now?'

Alfie sits back on the sofa and 'helps' me play.

Just as I've finished tooling up, a message appears saying the storm is closing in. I've never got this far before. I don't actually know what that means. What happens when the storm closes in? I'm assuming it's bad.

'I like storms,' says Alfie.

'Yeah, but you're weird,' I tell him.

'I know,' he says.

Then another message appears...

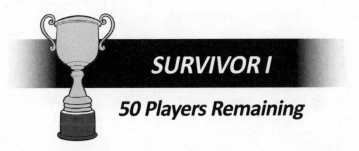

SURVIVOR I

50 Players Remaining

I'm in the top fifty! And I haven't even done anything yet!

What??

Now I get why Sana told me to stay on the bus until the end. This is like playing a totally different game.

A lot of players are impatient to land and get into the action.

Some players think being first to bail out of the bus means being first to the loot.

Some have got favourite places they like to go, where they know there are buildings with lots of loot to be found – maybe they're seeking out a special weapon.

Some just want to be in the middle of the map so they don't have to travel too far.

But! Because a lot of players do this, a lot of players end up really close together.

If you're a real hotshot at the game, that might not be a problem – maybe you're all about how many kills you can score in one match, in which case you want plenty of other players around.

But if you're a noob, it's a really good way to get knocked out in the first minute.

If you stay on the bus until the last few seconds – or just wait until the timer reaches zero and you get kicked out – you'll end up somewhere at the edge of the map.

Often you'll find you're the only one around, because everyone else is over the other side of the island, killing each other.

If you let the others wipe each other out, suddenly you've got a much better chance of winning!

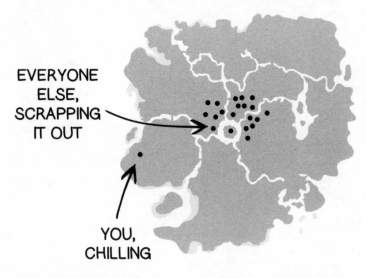

EVERYONE ELSE, SCRAPPING IT OUT

YOU, CHILLING

So now I've picked up some great gear, I want to use it! Alfie wants to see me make my first elimination and he's rocking back and forth on the sofa, getting over-excited. (Note to self: Don't let Alfie have drinks which contain caffeine.)

Look - another player running along a shore! He'll do. There's no way he's seen me so this should be easy. Come on, I can do this. I raise my hunting rifle -

Missed. By miles. This thing is hard to use. I reload –

But before I can even aim again, I'm eliminated. Someone just took me out from behind. I wonder if it's Sana, but it's just some random, picking up all my lovely loot.

But I placed #39! I've levelled up! I am officially Not A Total Noob! (I'm just Mostly A Noob.)

Alfie looks at me in awe. 'How did you do that?'

I explain my whole staying-on-the-bus strategy in full, except the part where I got it from Sana.

I go in for another match...

Now, Sana's strategy might not be for you. I won't be offended if you don't want to play that way, even though I just went to all this effort to explain it.

Landing away from other players means you'll see less action, and spend more of your time running around and hiding.

You might find it less exciting - especially if you get better at the game and feel you can take on other players.

Someone's got to survive those big shootouts, right? And it's cool if that player is you.

But playing more cautiously gives you a much better chance of placing high, and you can build up your XP without even having to fight anyone.

Searching loot crates and ammo crates earns XP, and you also get XP for surviving storm rounds. You even earn XP for hitting weak spots when harvesting materials - not much, but you do get some. And there are missions you can carry out to earn XP too.

Just like Minecraft! XP stands for eXperience Points...

well, sort of...

You also get to know your way around the map by playing this way, which really helps when you have to think fast and explore buildings quickly.

And think about how long you spend looking at loading screens, and in the lobby, and skydiving down... you want the actual match to last more than a couple of minutes, don't you?

Whatever strategy you're using, always check out the map before you jump. You can access it when you're in the lobby or while the battle bus is flying, and it'll show you the route of the bus.

This means you can work out where most of the other players will end up, and where the last stop will be.

Take a moment to think about exactly where you want to land - even if you're hanging on to the end, you'll have a few different choices. This gets easier after you've played a few matches, because the map gets filled in - and you can recognise and remember the buildings with good loot.

While the bus is flying, you can watch the back and get a general idea of where players are bailing out, and how many are bailing close to you.

If you can find a building that's got upgrading equipment, remember where it is and you can land there again!

Depending on how the match plays out, you may be able to hole up safely there for a while, and fill your time by harvesting materials and crafting yourself a better class of weapon.

I also worked out not to land on the ground.

The best way to search a building is to land on the roof, grab anything you can see, then smash your way down to the next floor and search that. Attics usually have chests in them, and often you can only get to them by breaking in.

This is also safer than running around on the ground, because in Fortnite it's better to be higher than your enemy.

Shooting downwards is easier than shooting upwards!

Buildings with flat roofs are good to find, because you're an easier target if you're standing on a sloping roof - but if you're landing away from other players that's less of a problem anyway.

Grab yourself a weapon just in case anyone has landed near you, and have it ready - when you're on the move, always keep a gun drawn rather than your harvesting tool or some bandages or whatever.

Never assume you're alone - and always watch the storm circle...

Oh yeah, and that is a good tip about thanking the bus driver. It's the down button in the chat controls. You get XP rewards for being polite!

CHAPTER 2

It's lunchtime next day.

I can see my mates again, over in the playground. I sort of want to go and talk to them - finally, I can join in a Fortnite conversation!

But... maybe Sana's told them about yesterday. And how she killed me. And my general noobishness. Maybe they're talking about that right now.

And if I go over there they'll all just laugh at me.

Maybe I'll hang out here, by the fence. Like in Fortnite - stay away from others, stay safe.

'Tyler, you bought your wristband yet?'

The voice comes from behind me. I had no idea there was anyone there.

I yelp. (Not that loudly, but you could definitely call it a yelp.)

I turn around and it's Maisie. She's our year's Events Rep. She never usually talks to me so I don't know why she's talking to me now.

'Sorry,' Maisie says, 'didn't mean to sneak up on you!'

'You didn't sneak up on me,' I say.

Maisie rattles a box of different-coloured wristbands. 'Well? Have you got yours yet?'

'What are they for?' I ask.

She rolls her eyes. 'The school disco, of course!'

'Oh,' I say. 'No.'

'Then it's lucky I came over, isn't it?' She points at the different colours.

'The green wristband is our basic package, with that you get access to the dancefloor and one soft drink and a hot dog... the purple wristband is the superior level and entitles you to all that plus a chocolate bar and a face-painting session... and the orange wristband is the elite pass which lets you use the VIP lounge...'

'There's different levels of wristband?' I say. 'Whose idea was that?'

'Mine!' she says proudly.

I don't know if I want to go to the disco anyway. I don't know how to dance. It's not my kind of thing. I'd rather be at home playing games.

'Sana's going,' Maisie adds with a sly little smirk.

'What?' I say. 'What difference would that make? Anyway I haven't got any money on me.'

'Bring it tomorrow. Next week all the prices are going up, so buy now if you don't want to pay more later!' She looks across at the playground, looking for more victims. 'Right, I need to hit my target of selling twelve wristbands every lunchtime, so –'

But just as I'm thinking, yes, please leave me alone... it starts raining.

I can see Sana and Ellie and Jake and Leon over on the playground, heading inside. But I'm OK here, sheltering under the big tree.

Until Maisie starts telling me all about her plans for the VIP lounge. She's bought a velvet rope and a curtain and she's got Big Naz to stand on the door and make sure nobody gets in without an orange wristband. There's going to be sushi and foot massages and...

I've got to get out of here. 'I'm going to run for it,' I tell Maisie.

'You'll get soaked,' she says.

Not if I run as fast as I can.

I can outrun the storm! I count 'One... two... three -'

Ten minutes later I'm sitting in the classroom in my PE kit while my clothes dry on the radiator.

Turns out that outrunning the storm was harder than it looked.

The shrinking map is an important part of Battle Royale games. At first the map needs to be big so that there's room for all the players. But when it gets down to the last few, the game forces players closer together so they can't camp out and wait for the other to attack.

In Fortnite this happens because of the storm.

The storm circle - that's the white circle where you're safe from the storm - appears after a few minutes and will keep getting smaller and smaller as the match goes on.

You might find you're already inside the storm circle when it appears. If so, lucky you - you can just stay there.

Use the building you started off in as your base. Go to the highest floor - that way, if enemies enter the building you'll hear them coming and can be ready for them.

Remember when you were on the battle bus and looked at the map to work out where everyone else was going to land? Well, they'll be coming from over there.

If you want to keep a lookout for them, you can find a window and look in that direction.

Or you can just find a good hiding spot and listen out for anyone approaching.

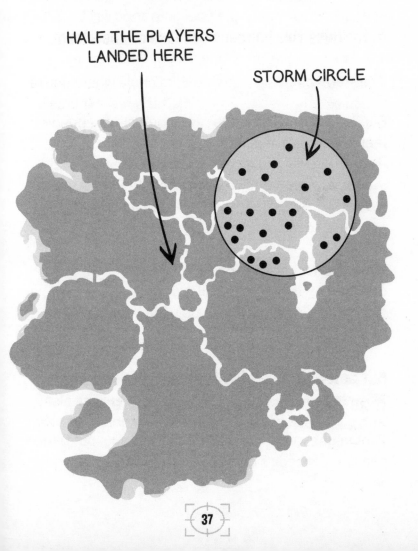

HALF THE PLAYERS
LANDED HERE

STORM CIRCLE

If you're not inside the storm circle, you're going to have to get over there before the storm closes in on you - so you can see why some people prefer to land in the middle of the map rather than the edges.

You never know where the storm circle's going to appear first, or where the final safe zone will be. If you land in one corner, and then the safe circle appears over on the other side, you'll have a really long way to go!

But don't worry - after the new storm circle appears, there's always enough time to get to safety. It just means you need to be quick about tooling up, and then start heading for the storm circle. This is one reason why it's a good idea to speed up your landing - you may need all the time you can get.

If the storm circle is a long way off, you might feel annoyed at having to run all that way. By the time you get to safety you'll probably have to start running again!

But actually, being the furthest player away from the storm circle can be a good thing.

That might sound like a dumb thing to say, but think about it - nobody's going to be sneaking up behind you and nobody's going to be running towards you. You're probably not going to get ambushed while you're picking up loot, and by the time you reach the storm circle, the competition will usually have thinned out a bit

Tyler Meeks! Where are you today? You haven't heard a word I've said, have you?

I have! I heard... those words you just said now. All of them.

Anyway... if you're at the edge of the storm circle, any players nearby are very likely to be moving in one direction – away from the storm... Be careful not to walk right into them!

If you want to stop running for a moment after getting to safety, get in a position where you've got a good view of anyone coming from that direction (without being seen yourself). Then you won't get any nasty surprises.

The position of the storm circle can tell you a lot about how other players will be moving. If the new storm circle appears right over on the west side of the old one, then think: Which way is everyone going to be moving? West.

So watch out for players coming from the east!

The storm should always be your main thought. If you're in danger of getting caught in the storm, don't stop to pick up loot. Don't even stop if you're under attack from other players! Just keep running.

Remember, you can't outrun the storm - if you stop for anything it'll catch you.

Don't stop to pick up the penny...

If another player hangs around shooting at you when the storm's closing in, you may find the storm gets rid of them. Problem solved!

As the storm circle gets smaller, you'll start to see where the endgame's going to take place. A match can play out very differently depending on where it ends up...

Anyway, I've managed to survive another day of school and made it home with a head full of Fortnite strategies. Let's go!

Me, playing Fortnite with lots of new ideas!

CHAPTER 3

Next morning I oversleep and it's already five minutes past eight. It's not my fault - I didn't get to sleep for ages last night, even though I went to bed at the usual time.

Uhh... what time is it?

Maybe I shouldn't have played that last match before bed. I do get a bit... hyped up.

Anyway, I'm trying to pack my bag but I start running around in a panic. I can't find my timetable and can't remember what lessons I've got today. I'm pretty sure it's Wednesday. Or Thursday.

No time to work out what I do and don't need - so I just chuck everything in. All my books, my art project, my PE kit, my swimming kit, my saxophone (they keep moving my lesson around so I can't keep track of when it is)...

Turns out that everything I ever need for school, if I put it all in one bag, is pretty heavy. It's taking me ages to walk to school, and I'm already running late...

And then -

SNAP!

My bag breaks.

I miss registration because of having to stop and put everything back in my bag, so I'm recorded late. And for the rest of the day I feel a few steps behind everything.

Like, at lunchtime I'm planning to avoid my mates again. But because I have to go via Lost Property to look for a bag I can carry everything home in, I'm at the end of the lunch queue –

And when I finally get my lunch, the only seat is on a table with Leon, Ellie and Jake. (Sana's at drama club.) It'll look weird if I don't sit with them.

'Nice bag, Tyler,' says Leon, pointing at the one I just got out of Lost Property. It's a backpack in the shape of a baby gorilla sucking its thumb.

THE OFFENDING BAG

'It was the only one I could find,' I mumble and sit down.

'What's your name then?' says Jake.

I blink at him, slowly. 'Tyler,' I say, pointing at myself. 'Is this some amazing joke? If it is, can you just skip to the end?'

Jake rolls his eyes. 'In Fortnite,' he says.

'Sana told us you started playing,' says Ellie.

Leon picks some food out of his teeth. 'I was playing a Duo match with Sana this morning before school...'

(Why does he always have to make sure everyone knows when he's been doing stuff with Sana? What's that about?)

'I asked her if you're any good,' Leon says.

'What did she say?' I reply, and I suddenly feel anxious. If she told them I'm good, that puts more pressure on me to be, y'know, actually good...

'No, she said you're hopeless.'

Ouch. That hurt.

Which is true. You can't count nothing, can you? 'But my XP level is 7, and I made Survivor II last night.' That's why I was up so late.

'What did you do?' asks Jake. 'Hide in a toilet? Did you hide in a toilet and just let the storm circle close in until someone found you?'

'Maybe,' I mutter through a mouthful of food.

As I walk home with my stupid gorilla bag, I think about how in Fortnite you also need to be careful about what you carry. Your inventory has five slots (not counting the one that's taken up by your harvesting tool), and they fill up quickly.

I played a game last night where I found loads of great weapons, and I didn't want to drop any of them, so I took them all... but I didn't make room for any medkits or bandages. That was a mistake.

Don't hoard stuff in your backpack and don't hang around wondering if you should drop this thing or that thing. Know what's in there and know what you can drop if you find something better.

And don't hang onto a weapon just because you went to the effort of upgrading it - if you find a better one, drop it!

Here's a rough idea of what to use your slots for (depends what you find, obviously)...

1. A GUN

An all-round weapon like an assault rifle is ideal - they're common, so you can probably find one. But if not, any gun will do.

2. A DIFFERENT GUN

Don't carry more than one of the same type of gun - after all, you can only use one at a time. A shotgun is a great secondary weapon, but if you can't find one, a pistol or a submachine gun is good - something that's effective at close range.

3. THROWING WEAPONS

Grenades, decoys, stuff like that.

4. HEALTH/SHIELDS

Food, bandages, medkits - or shield potions.

BANDAGES

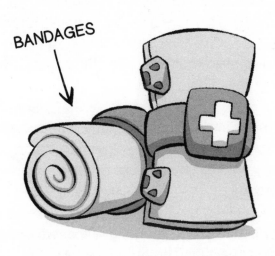

5. YOUR CHOICE

You could use this for a third gun, such as a sniper rifle, or one of the more unusual guns like a harpoon gun.

Or you can choose to carry medkits and shield potions - if you're using a sneaky strategy, you might prefer that.

Or carry decoys and grenades.

How you use your slots all depends on how you like to play.

If you're not great with throwing weapons, don't carry them - use the space for health, shield and a third gun.

You may also need that last space for a special item, like an upgrade table.

You don't need more than three guns. If you've got an assault rifle, a shotgun and a sniper rifle, that means you've got weapons you can use at close, medium and long range.

You don't need to carry a hunting rifle as well, or a submachine gun. If you prefer the pistol to the shotgun, carry it instead of the shotgun - don't carry both, unless there are no other weapons around of course.

Make sure you drink any shield potions you find immediately - as long as you're in a safe place and don't already have maximum shield. Topping up your shield is always a good move.

It also means that you can free up space in your inventory for other items that you might want or need.

You can stack items of the same type in your inventory, up to certain limits.

So for instance, if you've got fifteen bandages, you might feel it's not worth dropping them all for one medkit... but if you find more medkits later, you'll be able to stack them on that one.

(For some weird reason you can fit three medkits in your bag, but not one medkit plus five bandages. I didn't make up the rules.)

You also have slots for materials and ammo. But you can carry up to 999 of each type, which is more than you'll ever need so don't worry about it.

Loot can be found in chests, ammo boxes or just lying around.

Chests and ammo boxes are always in the same place on the map, so when you learn where they are, you can search an area more quickly.

AAAAAAAAAAAAAHHHHH....

LOOT CHEST

A standard chest always contains a weapon, the ammo for that weapon, some building materials and another item.

But in every match, there's a small chance that any chest will spawn as a rare chest, which is blue and guaranteed to contain at least a rare (blue) gun.

And maybe something better!

If you eliminate another player, you can grab their loot.

You also sometimes come across NPCs (non-playable characters) who will drop loot - they'll usually have decent weapons - and the sharks you'll encounter in the water will also drop loot when killed.

Supply drops fall during matches and are marked on the map. The quality of weapons in supply drops is very high - but you may run into other players going for the same loot.

Or worse, another player might be watching the drop with a sniper rifle, waiting for someone to come and find it!

Finally, you can find loot in supply llamas, which spawn in random locations.

These are packed with ammo, building materials, utility items - and traps you can set for other players!

SUPPLY LLAMA

Here's a rundown of items and what they do...

BANDAGES
These drop in stacks of five, you can carry up to 15 of them and they restore 15 health points each. (That's HP.) They're quick to use (three seconds) but can't bring your health above 75.

MEDKIT
Restores your health up to the full 100. The only drawback is it takes ten seconds to use, so use it when you're somewhere safe! ALWAYS use an inventory space for medkits if you find any.

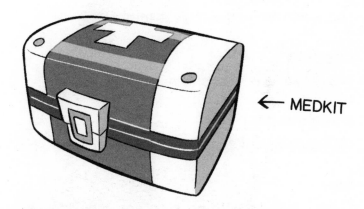

← MEDKIT

CHUG SPLASH
This is a throwable health item. Anyone who gets splashed by it gains 20 HP or shield. So if your squad are all together, you can throw this and all get the benefit.

FOOD

Food items can be found in shops or growing naturally.

Apples, bananas, coconuts, corn and peppers all heal five HP, up to a maximum of 100, and you can stack up to 15 of them.

CABBAGE

Not a fan of cabbage? Well, the makers of Fortnite have blatantly included this to troll you, because it's one of the best food items, restoring ten HP!

MUSHROOM

These add five to your shield, rather than HP.

COCONUT

These heal five HP or shield.

SLURPSHROOM

This special food item heals ten HP or shield.

FISH

There are three types of fish, which can be found in freezers or caught with a fishing rod. The small fry gives 25 HP, Flopper and Slurpfish 50 HP each.

FISHING ROD

For catching fish.. and maybe other stuff too.
If you're brave enough to stand around at the edge of
the water, making sploshy noises without your gun
drawn, grab one of these and go nuts. You can also
use them to ride sharks - if a shark grabs the bait, it'll
pull you through the water.

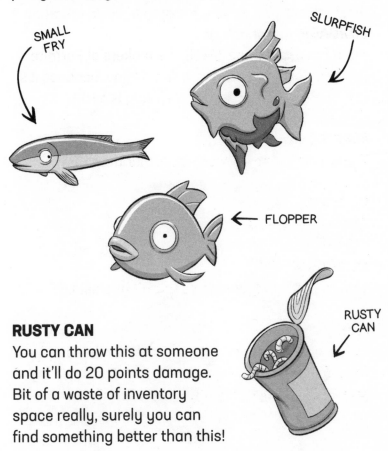

SMALL FRY

SLURPFISH

← FLOPPER

RUSTY CAN

You can throw this at someone
and it'll do 20 points damage.
Bit of a waste of inventory
space really, surely you can
find something better than this!

RUSTY CAN

SMALL SHIELD POTION

These are found in stacks of three and add 25 points to your shield, but you can't drink any if your shield is above 50.

SHIELD POTION

One of these adds 50 points to your shield, up to a maximum of 100. Having maximum shield is a huge advantage in a shootout.

← SHIELD POTION

SMALL SHIELD POTION ↓

CHUG JUICE ↑

SLURP JUICE (AN EPIC ITEM!) ←

If you have small shield potions and a shield potion, remember to drink the small ones first!

If you drink the regular shield potion first, you won't be able to drink the small ones.

So if you have time and space at the start of a match to explore a building, it can be worth checking if there are any small shield potions before you drink a regular one.

CRASH PAD

You can throw this on the ground and bounce off it. It's activated by pressing jump when you're already in the air - you don't need to select the item, just have it in your inventory.

They do deflate after a while.

LAUNCH PAD

This launches you into the air and your glider deploys again. It's handy for outrunning the storm. You need to place it on a built floor, and it can't be picked up again.

Launch pads can always be found in supply drops, so you can use them to make a quick getaway.

SHOCKWAVE GRENADE

GRENADE

DECOY GRENADE

STINK BOMB

GRENADE

The game's main throwing weapon, grenades deal 100 damage to enemies and 375 damage to structures. If you're hiding out in a building and other players are approaching, toss one of these out of the door!

DECOY

When you throw this, it creates a clone of you. This is great for drawing other players out of hiding, or for if you need to distract them while you escape.

STINK BOMB
When thrown, this creates a toxic cloud that deals five HP of damage every 0.5 seconds. Shields don't protect players against the damage.

UPGRADE BENCH
You can find upgrade benches scattered around the map, but they also appear as loot you can pick up.

Both types work the same way - you can use them to upgrade your weapons by feeding materials into them.

DON'T FORGET
The bench takes up an inventory slot which you really need for other stuff, so if you've got enough materials to upgrade one of your weapons, plant the table straight away and do the job.

You can't pick up the table once it's planted.

But you also probably won't have time to mess around upgrading weapons in the endgame, so the sooner you can do it, the better.

Okay, now I have exactly one hour and forty-two minutes of game time left today, which is enough for three good games...

or about a dozen bad ones.

GAME FACE

CHAPTER 4

I eliminated someone! OK, they'd just escaped from the storm and they were probably on about 4 HP but it still counts. Look, there it is on my stats. So proud.

Your Results			
★ Wins	0		
Top 10	0	Eliminations	1
Top 25	0	Matches Played	43

It seems stupid, but I feel a bit bad for whoever I eliminated. I wonder who it was. Probably some other noob who's always getting killed, just like me.

I'm really impatient to play with my mates now, so today at school I'm going to ask if I can do a squad match with them. They're always telling me I'm missing out by not playing, so they're going to say yes, right?

'Thing is...' says Leon, 'Squads are only four people.'

'And there's already four of us,' Ellie says.

'Yeah, I can count,' I tell her. 'But you don't always play together.'

'We do when we play Squads,' says Jake, shrugging.

'I could take a break,' says Sana. 'Give Tyler a turn -'

'I suppose you don't want to play with me because I'm so hopeless,' I say.

Sana looks a bit surprised. She shrugs. 'I don't mind, but whatever.'

'We could take a vote on it,' says Jake.

'Don't bother,' I say and walk off.

When I get home, I take out my frustration in Fortnite.

Or at least, that's the idea. It's not working out that way. I'm just getting killed over and over again, which is just making me more frustrated, which is... making me want to play more, for some reason.

'Shall we play something else?' says Alfie, who I'd sort of forgotten was there. He's brought his Switch round and is quietly playing his own games.

'I need to get good at this,' I tell him.

Just then, I get eaten by a shark.

'Yeah,' says Alfie, 'looks like that's going well.'

I turn to Alfie. 'It'd be better if you were helping me...'
What would be great would be if we could have a
Battle Lab session and I could use him for target
practice. But I don't want to tell him that.

'I'm not playing Fortnite,' he says without looking up
from his Switch.

'What are you playing?' I ask.

'Minecraft.'

And that gives me an idea. 'You can build in Fortnite.'

He glances up. 'Can you?'

'Yeah. We can build something together.'

'So I wouldn't have to shoot anything?'

'You wouldn't even have to carry a gun.'

He thinks about it. 'I don't see how Mum and Dad could get mad at me for that.'

The whole building bit of Fortnite is a bit unusual -
you don't normally get that in Battle Royale games,
but it comes from the original version of the game.

Like I said to you before, remember? The original game was about building a tower and escaping from zombies. That's why it's called FORTnite, geddit? You build forts.

AHHH... NOW I GET IT.

But I've noticed that the best Battle Royale players often have really good building skills, and it can make the difference between winning and losing a match.

There are three types of building material: wood, brick and metal. Sometimes they drop as loot, but you can also get them by smashing things up. Pretty much everything in the game, except for the ground and the water, can be smashed with your pickaxe for materials.

You can usually tell what an object will drop when smashed by looking at it: machinery, cars and fridges are metal; furniture is usually wood, and trees always are; brick drops from rocks and walls (although walls are often wood too).

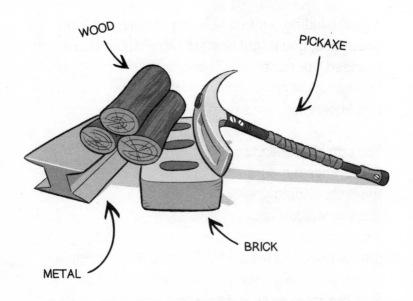

WOOD

PICKAXE

BRICK

METAL

Wood is the weakest material but it's quickest to build. Metal is strongest but slowest to build. Brick is medium strength and medium speed.

Wood is also the most common type of material. You tend to end up with some wood without even trying, just from smashing your way through buildings.

Being able to build is useful when you need to reach somewhere you can't reach any other way. As I said, some houses have an attic with no stairs up to it. Smash the ceiling and build stairs to get up there. You may also spot loot on roofs or mountain tops, which you can only reach by building.

If you're hiding out in a building that's had a wall destroyed, you might want to rebuild it so you're not exposed - or replace a broken floor to stop yourself falling. Just remember that other players will see it and know someone's been there!

You can also build to cross the map more quickly. Sometimes a mountain range is too steep for you to climb, forcing you to take the long way round. If the storm's coming, you might not have time - but if you've got quick building skills, you may be able to get round it that way.

But the main reason to build is defence.

Being able to put together a quick fortress can be a life-saver. And by 'quick' I mean 'not staring down at your controller trying to remember which button makes stairs'.

By the time you've remembered you might be too dead to make any stairs.

Like I said, Battle Lab is great for practising your building. Alfie and I had a competition to see who could make a five-storey fort quickest.

Alfie won. But I didn't mind.

It's all part of my secret plan to get him into the game. (Don't tell Alfie there's a secret plan to get him into the game. But look, he's installed the game, he's created an account, he's in my friends list... I'll wear him down yet.)

One thing to remember is that when you're building, you don't have your weapon drawn – which is risky. A bit of practice switching between building and weapons pays off.

It's not worth building anything complicated early in the match, because if it's not inside the storm circle you'll have to leave it behind. And in the early stages you'll just draw attention to yourself by building a big fort – everyone will know you're there.

There are some defensive building skills that can be useful when you're moving across the map though. If someone's shooting at you and you're not sure where they are, throwing up a quick wall is a good skill to have.

If you're under attack you need to build quickly, so use wood.

Once your cover's in place, you need to be able to fire back at the enemy. You could peek around the side of the wall – or you can use the edit function to add a window or door. This is an underrated tactic, but only use it if you've got a bit of breathing space!

You can build stairs instead of walls - they don't offer such good cover, so only use them if you know where the enemy is.

Make the stairs a few storeys high and you can climb them (crouch if you want to keep out of sight) and use your height advantage to fire back at the enemy. With a bit of practice this tactic can really surprise opponents.

Just make sure nobody's running up behind you!

Whether you need to build in the endgame depends on where the storm circle closes in.

Sometimes it's around an existing building and you can find some good cover there without having to build. (Again, this avoids drawing attention.)

But sometimes the endgame happens out in the open, and that's when you need to think about forts.

If the other remaining players are attacking, build with wood for speed. But if you do have a little time, brick and metal are better at this stage.

Don't waste materials!

A high fort is better than one that covers a wide area
- you only need enough cover to hide behind and
height is always an advantage.

But don't make it too high, because if someone blows
it up the fall could kill you.

Once your fort is in place, your opponents may try to break it down by firing at it. Remember you can repair walls by highlighting them.

If they're broken, you can rebuild a wall as soon as it's been demolished - you'll need to be super-quick at building, and also use wood for this. This can make your opponent waste loads of ammo, so it's good to learn.

If it comes down to you and one or two other players holed up in your forts, waiting for the others to come out and attack - it may come down to luck, and whoever's fortress ends up inside the storm circle while the others are forced to move.

Alfie wouldn't be much use at that stage of the game. But it's fun finally getting to play with someone else!

CHAPTER 5

I'm hiding out in a wooden shack on a hill, there's nineteen players left including me - and I'm at the centre of the storm circle. I don't have to move anywhere - just wait for the others to come to me. I've got a hunting rifle ready for when they do.

It's all pretty tense.

'Can you wash your hands?' Mum says. 'Dinner's nearly ready.'

I've tried to make Mum understand that Fortnite isn't like the games she played when she was my age, and that when a match has started you can't just pause it and pick it up again later.

'In a minute,' I tell her.

Five minutes go by. The storm circle keeps closing in and I'm still in the middle. Twelve players left.

I'm about to make Survivor III for the first time!

Dad sticks his head in the room. He looks a bit annoyed. 'Dinner is on the table,' he says.

'I'm just in the middle of –' I start to say.

'Well, you're going to have to not be in the middle of,' he says. 'Are you playing that game again?'

I pretend not to know what 'that game' means so I don't have to tell him I am. He heads downstairs.

I look down at the screen. Eleven players left. If I can just hang on for a minute...

I take my Switch into the bathroom and prop it on top of the toilet while I wash my hands. I decide to take my time over it and wash them really, really well. Clean down the sides of my fingernails and everything.

'Tyler!' comes a shout from downstairs: Mum again.

'I'm washing my hands!' I shout back.

'You should have washed them ten minutes ago when I asked you!'

'Okay, okay...'

Then I see an orange flash on the screen of the Switch. My shack's on fire! Argh! I quickly dry my hands and pick up the Switch –

But it's no good. I'm dead.

Someone called **DaBesst99** killed me with a flare gun.

Of course, when I get to the table there's a lecture about coming to eat when I'm told, and how they think I'm playing far too much Fortnite, and have I done my homework?

(And yes I have done it, well... most of it.)

And they don't like how grumpy I get after I've been playing.

(I only get grumpy because I'm not very good at it, if I played more then I'd get good and I wouldn't be grumpy).

I'm not really listening. I don't need to because I know what they're saying anyway. I'm thinking about flare guns.

Like, what are flare guns?

I've found them before but didn't really know what they did, so I left them and picked up other weapons instead.

I need to find out more about weapons.

There are so many weapons in Fortnite - how are you supposed to know which ones are best?

The first thing to understand is the colour-coding system, because I didn't find this obvious at all when I started.

All weapons have a coloured glow around them, and the colour tells you how good the weapon is..

GREY = COMMON

GREEN = UNCOMMON

BLUE = RARE

PURPLE = EPIC

ORANGE = LEGENDARY

GOLD = MYTHIC

The **ASSAULT RIFLE** is the staple weapon of any Fortnite player. It's a good all-rounder, can be used at any distance and is pretty accurate.

The basic Assault Rifle - which you can find in grey, green, blue, purple or orange - is a great weapon to have.

The purple and orange assault rifle is quite a bit more accurate than the lower grades, so if you get a chance to upgrade yours - do it!

There's also a Burst Assault Rifle (in grey, green, blue, purple, orange, gold) which fires off two rounds at a time.

One stupid thing I did when I started playing Fortnite was I assumed if any weapon had an extra word to describe it, it MUST be better than a weapon without -

like how toffee popcorn is better than just popcorn!

POPCORN

TOFFEE
POPCORN

But actually the burst assault rifle isn't as accurate as the basic one. It's good at short range but generally you're better off with the normal assault rifle.

PISTOLS AND MACHINE GUNS are the weakest guns available, BUT they're effective at close range and fire quickly.

If you find yourself preparing an ambush, or trying to take out an enemy who's hiding and thinks you don't know they're there, one of these will come in useful.

The basic automatic pistol (which comes in grey, green, purple or orange) deals pretty low damage, but has high accuracy – especially the purple and orange variants. If you find one of those, it's worth hanging onto.

The basic Submachine Gun (also in grey, green, blue, purple, orange) is known as an SMG. It has a rapid rate of fire and good accuracy, but actually it doesn't do much damage.

It's useful over near-to-medium distances where you don't have much time to aim.

Just scatter bullets and hope you hit someone!!

SHOTGUNS are the second most useful weapon in the game, especially for noobs - they're close-range weapons that don't need to be accurately aimed, and are ideal indoor and street weapons.

The Tactical Shotgun (grey, green, blue, purple, orange) has a quick fire rate. If you're holed up in a room somewhere, this is a brilliant weapon to have - keep it trained on the door and be ready to shoot anyone who enters.

The purple and orange variants do significantly more damage to buildings, forts and other strucutres.

If you want to deal out more damage than a tactical shotgun, you could try the Charge Shotgun (grey, green, blue, purple, orange or gold - with the purple and orange ones doing over 90 points!)

This weapon reloads slightly quicker than the Tactical Shotgun- but its fire rate is slower, making it better for slightly more experienced players who are confident of hitting the target.

You can also look out for **SNIPER RIFLES** which are designed for long-range shooting. They can do a lot of damage but the downside is that they can only take one bullet at a time, so they need to be reloaded between shots and should only be used when you have time and cover.

There's a real art to using these things... which sadly I don't have, but I'm learning.

The Hunting Rifle (green, blue, orange, purple) is a variation which can be tricky to use – it doesn't have a telescopic sight, so you have to aim it like you would any other gun.

But it's pretty accurate and very powerful and a headshot from a hunting rifle will take out an opponent – the orange version deals out 100 points damage!

Finally, there's the Bolt-Action Sniper Rifle (which you can find in blue, purple and orange).

This rifle does more damage than pretty much any other weapon I can think of – if the opponent has no shields you can kill them with one bullet, without even needing to make a headshot.

A single clean headshot from the bolt-action sniper will also down an enemy with full shields. Its telescopic sight is great, but it's a slow weapon to use, so it may not be for everyone.

I've also come across a few other guns, which don't neatly fit the other categories...

The Flare Gun (which is blue) holds six flares and deals out 60 points of damage.

Fires breakout wherever the flares land... and these can reveal your opponents' positions!

This weapon is great for the endgame, especially if your opponent has made a fort for themselves out of wood.

(Exactly what **DaBesst99 did to me in that last match. Grr... And what I am definitely planning to do myself as soon as the opportunity arises.**)

Flare up and burn it down!

It's very rarely found, but if you can get your hands on a Rocket Launcher (in either purple or orange) you can inflict A LOT of damage - especially to structures.

If you know someone's hiding inside a building, the Rocket Launcher is just what you need!

Maybe I'll try that next time.

The Shockwave Launcher comes in gold so it's a mythic weapon, which basically means it is especially rare or powerful.

The Shockwave Launcher doesn't do much actual damage to an opponent, instead it flings players around, which can give you an advantage or buy you some time.

If you're looking for something weird but useful, keep your eyes open for the Harpoon Gun (a blue level weapon)

It shoots out a hook on a rope, so you can use it to pull things towards you, including enemies. It does a lot of damage to structures if you use it this way. And you can fish with it.

You can even hook a shark and get it to pull you along the water!

If you're using the harpoon gun against an opponent then it's best at medium and close range - I once got attacked right after landing and this was all I'd managed to pick up.

A clean headshot took my opponent straight out!

Then I got snipered by someone else.

But for a moment I felt like a **BEAST**.

WORST TO BEST

* Pistol
* SMG
* Tactical Shotgun
* ~~Burst Assault Rifle~~
* Hunting Rifle
* Burst Assault Rifle
* ~~Flare Gun~~
* ~~Charge Shotgun~~
* Harpoon Gun
* Flare Gun
* Charge Shotgun
* Assault Rifle
* Drum Gun

So the next day, I'm in class, waiting for the register to be taken and writing out my Absolutely Complete Hierarchy Of Fortnite Weapons.

This is going to be pretty useful.

Wait, I forgot the Bolt-Action Sniper Rifle.

Hmmm... Where can that go?

And is an Uncommon Pistol better than a Common Assault Rifle?

Just then, Leon walks past my desk.

'Hot last night, wasn't it?' he says.

I look up. 'Not especially.'

'You didn't get too hot? Round about six o'clock?'

'No.' What is he talking about?

'Just thought you might have got *burned*.'

Then I remember: the flare gun!

I point at him.

Leon doesn't say anything. He just winks and walks on to his own desk. I can see Ellie and Jake sitting at the back of the room, laughing at me.

I turn back to the front, seething – and Maisie's there, rattling her stupid box of disco wristbands in three different colours.

'Did you bring your money in today?' she says, smiling.

'I'm not coming to the dumb disco, Maisie,' I snap at her.

Maisie puts her hands on her hips. 'Do not call my disco dumb.'

'I will call your dumb disco dumb if I think it's dumb, and I do.'

Maisie stomps away.

I don't want to think about the disco. I don't want to think about anything else. Not even any other games.

It's Fortnite all the way from now on, until I've got revenge on Leon!

CHAPTER 6

'Do you want any more Fortnite tips?' says Sana when we're walking through the gates at the end of school.

'Not from you,' I say. She's probably just looking to get more funny stories about how hopeless I am so she can tell the others.

'What's wrong with you?'

'Nothing,' I say, and walk the other way, heading for home.

This is one of those moments when you need a friend who already knows you're hopeless, and who won't tell anyone about it because there's no-one he can tell...

But Alfie doesn't want to play.

'You played before,' I say.

'Only to build forts.'

'You can build forts now. You don't have to fight.'

'But isn't that the only way you can win, by fighting?'

'Yeah, but you'll still be helping me - you can build the forts for me. And it'll mean there's one less person trying to kill me.'

Alfie looks at the floor. 'You never want to play anything else these days.'

'If you do this I'll play whatever you want afterwards. Please.'

He thinks about it for a bit. I'm like the devil on his shoulder.

You know you want to play a Battle Royale, deep down...give in...

Alfie sighs. 'Alright.'

Alfie and I decide to play Duos and we find a match. We agree we're both going to do the stay-on-the-bus thing, land together and stick together.

And also, Alfie's going to do what I say.

And I get all the best weapons and ammo, since he's not going to use any.

After a couple of minutes we need to move towards the storm circle, and I tell Alfie he's going to have to stop smashing up the house we started off in.

He's playing it like it's Minecraft. Half of the walls are gone.

'Be careful doing that,' I tell him. 'You don't want to attract attention.'

'Alright,' he says, and we head across the map.

When my inventory fills up, but I still want to carry stuff, Alfie says he'll carry it for me.

'I'm like your squire,' he says.

'What's a squire?'

'Knights had them in mediaeval times. A squire carried the knight's weapons and stuff so they didn't weigh him down when he was fighting.'

'Oh yeah. Do you mind being a squire?'

'It's cool.'

If he thinks it's cool, who am I to argue?

We make a good team, and we're down to Survivor II when I see another player running between two buildings. I don't think it's Leon, but I'm not sure what he looks like...

'Take cover!' I tell Alfie, and run at the enemy. I get a couple of good shots in before she sees me, but she's got a legendary assault rifle from somewhere and she eliminates me.

Gah!

'Are you dead?' Alfie says.

'Yeah, but I think you can revive me.'

'How?'

'Dunno,' I'm switching to spectate mode so I can see what he's doing. 'Where are you?'

'In a building.'

'Have you got any guns?'

'Er... a green pistol.'

'Is that all?'

'Yeah. Is that rubbish?'

'Yes.'

'Oh.'

The storm circle moves. It's getting small now, and Alfie has to move.

He heads for the centre, the top of a hill, and starts building a tower.

I don't have the heart to tell him it's pointless. He's got no shields and he's never even fired a weapon in the game. As soon as anyone finds him he's done for.

I notice there's only seven players left.

Alfie finishes his fort. It's pretty impressive. He sits at the top of it and waits.

Four players left. The circle shrinks again... but Alfie's still inside it.

One of the other remaining players, someone called **NuttyBoyeee13**, takes out two of the others. Alfie is in the top two?

Alfie sits tight at the top of his tower. We wait. And wait.

Then we wait some more.

At the side of the screen I see:

NuttyBoyeee13 was lost in the storm

Wait... it can't be. Surely? But then a message appears:

#1 VICTORY ROYALE

'What does that mean?' Alfie asks innocently.

'It means,' I say as calmly as I can, 'that you won.'

'Won what?'

'The match. You won.'

'Oh brilliant. How though?'

'The others all killed each other, and then the last one got killed by the storm.'

Alfie smiles. 'That's funny, isn't it? I won first time and I didn't even kill anyone.'

I grit my teeth.

'Yes. It's very, very funny that you've fluked a Victory Royale in the game I've spent all week trying to get good at.'

'Exactly!' says Alfie.

So what happened with Alfie is annoying but it's made me realise something about Fortnite, which is that some of the best advice on fighting is - don't!

OK, fighting is a big part of the fun and making eliminations does earn XP, so you'll want to do some fighting at some point. But if you just run around looking for people to kill, you'll probably get killed yourself pretty quickly.

When you walk around shooting anything that moves, you're letting everyone know exactly where you are.

There'll always be some players who just want to go wild and cause as much mayhem as possible before they get taken out.

Let them!

The more people they eliminate, the fewer people you'll have to deal with.

Avoid getting into combat if you don't need to. After that last match I realised I didn't need to go and attack that player who eliminated me.

Sure, if someone ambushes you, or if you run into each other and there's nowhere to go, get shooting!

But if someone doesn't know you're there, don't run at them with guns blazing just because you can - especially if their position is good.

Wait and see what they do. Someone else might get rid of them for you.

Or the storm might force them to move.

Or they might get bored waiting and come out into the open just to make something happen.

Fortnite rewards players who are patient and don't get bored when everything goes quiet!

If you do what I've been doing and land away from other players, you might not see anyone else for ages. When you do, don't get over-excited and rush to fight them!

Think about whether you **really need** to fight this person, or whether you can just give them a wide berth.

Hopefully your starting point will be inside a building on your own - stay there until the storm circle appears.

If you have to move, find the nearest building that's inside the storm circle and hide out there.

Avoid the open as much as you can.

You can make your way across the map pretty safely by moving this way.

Of course, when you enter a building, you need to remember another player might already have grabbed it for their own hideout!

Whenever you enter a building, look out for:

* **open doors**

* open chests

* open ammo boxes

* structures built by players

* missing wall

If you see any of those things, go carefully in case anyone's hiding there.

Hopefully they'll have already been and gone.

If you're lucky there's been a huge battle and the winner has already moved on, leaving loads of dropped loot for you to pick up.

When it gets to the endgame, there'll come a point where you can't avoid the others any more.

Either they'll come looking for you, or the storm will push you close together.

But by then you'll probably place pretty highly.

And if you get mega lucky like Alfie, you might even win a Victory Royale by waiting it out.

There are several ways to die in Fortnite, and if your opponents don't get caught in the storm, they might fall from a great height, or get killed by a shark, or get eliminated by an NPC (which is short for a non-playable character).

I've decided to let Alfie be happy with his Victory Royale. I mean, technically it's mine too, because we were playing as a team. It's there on my stats.

But it doesn't feel proper.

I need a real one...

CHAPTER 7

The next day at school, I've been roped into helping to clear out the art cupboard - a leaky water pipe has turned a load of craft paper into mush, and I'm taking it to be recycled. I walk past an open window that overlooks the playground...

And I see Leon standing down below, with his back to me. He's talking to Maisie. I think he's already bought a wristband, so she must be pushing him to upgrade. He looks like he wants to walk away, but Maisie won't let him.

Without even thinking about what I'm doing, I reach into the bag of mushed-up paper, get a piece of it out and crumple it into a ball.

Then making sure I'm ready to duck down... I get Leon in my sights, take aim and launch the soggy missile directly at my unsuspecting opponent...

It connects with a satisfying SLOMP noise, right on target, so that the water trickles down his neck and the paper leaves a satisfying smudge on the back of his shirt.

Maisie yelps and dodges back!

I'd love to stop and see his face when he turns around - but I drop below the level of the window and make do with listening to Leon shout

'WHO WAS THAT?'

and accuse random kids standing nearby.

Feeling pretty pleased with myself for seeing the opportunity, the tactical position and using some serious stealth and accuracy, I stay out of sight, pick up the bag of paper and walk on.

Then pushing aside a flicker of guilt, I turn my mind back to the problem of **DaBesst99**.

You see, the tricky thing about getting good at fighting in Fortnite is that you don't get much chance to learn.

When you get into combat situations there's hardly any time to think and you can't just **pause the game** while you figure out what to do next!

By then you'll be dead.

This is another reason to stay out of sight and not rush into combat.

If you see other players coming before they see you, that gives you a little more time to work out your strategy.

Different players will fight differently, so unfortunately there's no advice that works for every situation - you really need to learn to think on your feet and react quickly.

Another thing I've just discovered - did you know you can adjust the sensitivity of your controls?

I found this out when when I was mucking about in the settings menu after losing ANOTHER match.

The default is pretty sensitive, so when you try to aim, your sights will swing around a lot.

This can make it hard to aim when you're in a hurry, especially if you're like me - I get really edgy when I'm going into combat and I tend to press the controls hard.

So another player will be running at me and I'm trying to aim at them but I keep shooting either side.

Fortnite avatars are narrow targets!

You don't want your aim to move too slowly, but if you can slow it down a bit, it can really help you find the target. All those other players who seem to have a much sharper aim than you might just have spent more time tweaking their settings.

There isn't a 'right' setting. Ask pro Fortnite players what setting they use and you'll get lots of different answers.

You need to find what works for you - so try it out before you play a proper match. Alfie and I did an hour in the Battle Lab so I could tweak my settings. He ran around for an hour while I shot at him.

That's a true friend right there.

Also, Fortnite is very different depending on whether you play on a computer with a keyboard and mouse, or a console.

A lot of top players use keyboard and mouse, because the keyboard doesn't need to be toggled between building and combat controls, and the mouse is more accurate when aiming.

If you're using a computer, getting a good quality mouse is a good move, especially if you're playing on a laptop with a built-in trackpad – that's a better way to spend money than on in-game items which make you look good but won't give you any playing advantage!

If you're playing on a console like me, do what you can to tune up your Fortnite experience.

You can change your controller settings. There are a few different presets, but you can also make your own custom set-up.

Over the years, feedback from players means the default settings are mostly the best ones – but you may find you want quicker access to something, like the Edit or Repair features.

If you do make any changes to the settings don't forget to try them out in a practice situation before you go into a proper match!

I find pressing down on the thumbsticks isn't very precise when I'm in a hurry, and I don't use the D-buttons much for chatting – so I like to use one of those buttons for crouching.

Hang on... I forgot I changed the button to make me jump!

Crouching is an important tactic to master. As well as the obvious - it means you can hide more easily - you don't make noise when you move around while crouching.

This is especially important if you find yourself moving around a building and you know there are other players in there.

Sound travels through buildings very easily so anything that keeps you out of sight AND keeps you quiet is definitely a plus.

NPCs are also easily attracted by noise, and will come after you if they notice you moving through their territory. Fighting NPCs won't win you the match, and it's risky - so it's better to just avoid them. Move quietly through their territory if you can.

Though sometimes you may need to just run for it!!

When running, it's tempting to go in a straight line because it's the quickest way to get where you're going - whether that's safe cover or the storm circle.

But it makes you easier to hit. If you think there could be someone targeting you, run in a slight zigzag.

It won't slow you down that much and will make you a lot harder to hit!

If there's someone running up behind you, or hiding upstairs in that building you're heading for, they could be lining up a nice clear headshot with a sniper rifle, and then you've had it.

So if you can, try to avoid close combat and combat out in the open. If they can spot you out and about, then skilled players will run rings around you and shoot you before you even get a chance to aim!

One of the most annoying things is when you go to fire at someone, and just when you've got your aim right, you run out of bullets and are left standing there like an idiot while you reload.

Get used to reloading before going into combat, and master the art of ducking behind cover so you can reload without being shot at.

(That's another good reason to avoid close combat: cover won't do you much good if your opponent is close enough to walk around it and shoot you while you're reloading or healing.)

You can make up for a lack of combat skills by using surprise. You can try hiding out in buildings and ambushing other players.

As you move through the map look out for a room that you can hole up in - ideally on one of the upper floors, and without windows.

If you're upstairs, you're more likely to hear opponents coming - their footsteps will echo up from the ground floor and you'll hear them coming up the stairs.

Make sure you close the door behind you, so it looks like the room hasn't been explored yet, and find a position where you can see the door.

If there are windows, try to keep away from them.

The ideal weapon for this situation is a shotgun, because you're almost guaranteed to hit the target at this range - but an assault rifle, pistol or machine gun will do.

Make sure your gun is loaded.

Think about where your opponent will be when they walk through the door - this is your chance to get a headshot! - and train your gun on it.

And then wait....

Maybe no-one will walk in. But if they do, you're ready for them.

Just remember to pay attention to the walls, especially if you're on the ground floor - someone might be bashing them down or shooting them up, and then you'll have to switch your aim.

Ideally - if you don't make any noise - the opponent won't know you're there and you can surprise them.

But ambush tactics can also work even if an opponent knows you're there and has gone into the building to find you.

Often, this kind of opponent will try to corner you if you run away.

But if you can get into a room before they reach you, you can turn and train your gun on the doorway.

If there's only one way they can get into the room, there's only one place you need to aim!

In Fortnite headshots do more damage to your opponent, but only try headshots if you've got time to pick your target - if you're trying to hit a moving player, or if you're using a less accurate weapon, then you're much better off aiming for the body.

Of course, other players will be aiming for your head too - and some players are very good at getting their aim at the right level. Crouching can really put them off, and it makes you a smaller target - though you can't move as fast.

Running past other players while firing is also a a good tactic to master - **if you run at them they'll get a clear shot!**

As I've said before, in combat it's always better to be higher than your opponent. The main reason for this is headshots. If you're looking down on your opponent, you can see more of their head - and they can see less of yours.

This height gives you an advantage, so use it!

And it doesn't even have to be a big height advantage.

If you're in a room plotting an ambush, and there's something you can stand on like a desk, a bed or a crate, go for it. When the other player walks in, it'll take them a moment to adjust to you being higher up and you can get your own shot away.

You can also get a height advantage by doing jump shots.

This is when you fire at another player while jumping in the air.

These sort of shots are tricky to master, but they're good for the following reasons:

* **You increase your chance of headshot**
* **It's hard for others to hit you when you're jumping around**
* **It confuses opponents and you can strike at them while they work out what the flip's going on!**

The only real problem with jump shots is that is can be quite hard for you to aim at others, while you're bouncing up and down....

And if you jump repeatedly your jumps get lower each time, and you need to rest.

If you are planning on jumping, make sure you have some nearby cover, or jump out from behind cover.

When you're hiding, of course you need to keep a lookout for other players. But remember that in Fortnite, what you see on the screen isn't your character's point of view.

It's possible to position your character just behind a bit of cover, while angling the camera in a way that means you, the player, can see around the edge of the cover.

You can also use this when entering new areas to avoid getting ambushed.

If the enemy isn't being careless or gung-ho, you can end up in a standoff. You're safely behind your cover and they're safely behind theirs.

How can you draw them out of hiding?

If you know where they're hiding, and they're within range, you can use a weapon like a grenade or flare gun to damage their cover.

The flare gun is especially useful in destroying other players' wooden forts, as it sets fire to them. (This is a lesson I will NOT be forgetting easily.)

A more advanced tactic is to use decoys.

It's a bit of a risk to carry decoys around, because they're only useful in certain situations and there are more versatile weapons you can carry. But they're very useful for drawing out enemies when you don't know where they're hiding.

Wait for the enemy to shoot at the decoy, then watch and listen for where the gunfire is coming from.

If you're playing a Duos or Squads match, and at least two of you are left at the end, one of you can run at the enemy while the other one watches to see where they are - or attacks the enemy from a different angle.

Obviously this is risky - if one of you gets eliminated doing this, you don't get another chance!

But if it's two of you against one opponent, and all you have to do to win is eliminate them, it might be worth it.

It's incredibly hard to tackle two opponents at once in Fortnite, so while the enemy is distracted taking one of you down, the other one should get a chance to strike.

But this is the value of keeping teammates alive to the end. It's not such an advantage early on, but it's massive in the endgame. The problem is agreeing which of you's going to run out and get shot at and which of you is going to do the shooting...

Lucky for me - I know someone called Alfie who wouldn't have a problem with that at all...

CHAPTER 8

So I've told Alfie exactly what to do: play exactly like he did before, stick with me, try to get to the endgame, and I'll tell him when it's time to go out and run around.

If he wants to think that, fine. Whatever.

I've decided to play a Squads match. Alfie and I fill two of the four slots, and the other two get filled by random players called **6DogTag8** and **LandsEnder500**.

When the Battle Bus sets off, I see a familiar name pop up:

Dabesst99 has thanked the bus driver

'Who? What?' says Alfie.

'One of my "friends" from school is in this match,' I explain.

'That's nice.'

'Didn't you hear the quote marks around "friends" just then?'

'Oh, sorry. No.'

I wonder where Leon bailed out. I hope we run into him... but not just yet.

Alfie and I land together and stick together, like we did last time. We land well away from everyone else and build up plenty of loot, like last time.

I've got a shotgun, assault rifle and sniper rifle. Alfie's carrying chug splashes, a harpoon gun, shield potions and a pistol for emergencies which he insists he's not going to use.

The storm circle appears. 'It's miles away,' says Alfie.

'That's OK,' I tell him. 'This all fits with my strategy.'

WHAT ARE YOU DOING OVER THERE?

'What was that voice?' Alfie asks.

I forgot - when you play Squads you can talk to other members of your squad if you turn on your microphone.

Alfie doesn't have his turned on and neither do I - I'm afraid of saying something stupid, and also I'm afraid of Alfie saying something stupid.

But someone else on our squad, **6DogTag8**, does have his turned on. He sounds about our age, maybe a little bit older.

'Do we answer him?' says Alfie. 'Where's the chat window?'

'No,' I say. 'We need to keep moving, don't stop to chat. Just ignore him.'

'OK, we'll ignore him.'

Then he lands in front of us in a helicopter.

'Whaaa...?' Alfie's confused because he hasn't seen vehicles in the game yet.

I'm annoyed because this isn't my strategy.

I want to move stealthily, and the helicopter is **literally the loudest way to move around in this game.**

But on the other hand, we are a long way from the storm circle, and we'll get there much quicker this way.

And it seems rude to say 'No thanks, we'll walk.'

So we hop onto the helicopter and it lifts us up and away.

All sorts of vehicles spawn in various places around the Fortnite map, but they don't spawn randomly - they appear in places that fit with the type of vehicle they are.

So you might find a helicopter on a military base, or speedboats at a marina.

They mostly come in useful when you need to get across the map quickly, like when you need to outrun the storm, or get away from a bunch of NPCs who just won't leave you alone.

The downside of travelling this way is you don't find as much loot. So while your teammates may be trying to help by picking you up, it can be annoying if you have no shields and rubbish weapons and really need to find some more stuff.

Vehicles come equipped with their own weapons, which the driver can operate, and any passengers can use whatever weapons they've got with them.

It's not a subtle way of attacking opponents, because they will hear you coming - but if you're handy with long-range weapons, you'll never have a better height advantage than the one you get from the helicopter.

But don't hang onto a vehicle for too long!

They're only useful when the playing area is still big. As it shrinks, the advantage of being able to move across it quickly also shrinks - and they really draw attention to you.

Ditch your vehicle well before the endgame and find some cover - you really don't want other players to see you rock up in a speedboat...

... you'll be an easy target when you hop out and run for the nearest building.

If you've never used a vehicle before, you can do a Battle Labs session to work it out so you don't crash into a mountain in the middle of a match.

You can also learn where the vehicles spawn so you can head for one if you decide you need one in a game situation.

I'm expecting our new pal **6DogTag8** to fly us to the storm circle - but he doesn't.

I don't know what's going on now.

My strategy has gone totally out of the window.

I notice the fourth member of our squad, **LandsEnder500**, has been eliminated.

Well, at least we lasted longer than her.

The helicopter lands, we all get out - and I blunder straight into a floating computer chip thing.

I've picked up **LandsEnder500's** reboot card, apparently.

'Get to the reboot van,' says **6DogTag8**, over the voice chat, 'I'm going to look for loot.'

'What do I do?' I ask Alfie.

'You're the expert,' Alfie says.

'I'm really not.'

There's a reboot van nearby and I work out what I'm meant to do.

When a teammate is eliminated you've got 90 seconds to pick up their reboot card. If you take it to a reboot van you can bring your teammate back.

They won't have any of their old loot - they'll have dropped all that - so it's handy if you have enough loot to share some with them.

Luckily, we've got Alfie with us, so he gives her some shield potions and materials.

LandsEnder500 is very grateful, and pings us a friend request. But we don't have time for that now.

Back to the choppa!

6DogTag8 takes us all the way to until the heart of the storm circle, and we land on top of a tall building.

I really don't know how this is going to work. I've never played a match this way.

Alfie and I agree to hide in a room somewhere. We find one with no windows and shut ourselves inside.

There's a desk in the corner, so I go and stand on it. Alfie stands on it with me.

There's gunfire outside: our teammates are getting into combat.

LandsEnder500 is eliminated. Again.

Alfie and I have a moment of silent respect for her.

The storm circle shrinks.

We've got to move – but I tell Alfie to wait a moment.

There's still gunfire outside.

Any second now they'll all move towards the storm circle, and if we wait for them to go, we won't run straight into them.

Thirty seconds later, we open the door and rush out – and I notice **6DogTag8** has been eliminated in the firefight.

'Get my reboot card!' he says into his microphone.

'Should we?' Alfie asks me.

But I can see we don't have time.

We've only just got time to reach the storm circle, we can't stop...

Alfie and I run out of the building, away from our fallen comrade.

He isn't happy.

COME BACK HERE AND PICK UP MY ~~#*&%~~ REBOOT CARD AND PUT ME BACK IN THE GAME YOU ~~*&%*%*%~~ LOSERS!!!!!

'Er... I'm going to turn down the volume,' says Alfie.

'No, don't,' I tell him. 'You need your sound on or they'll sneak up on you - there must be a way to mute him.'

I quickly click on the menu and look for an option to do it...

But while I'm fiddling with the settings and trying to mute him, I hear gunfire –

I've been eliminated.

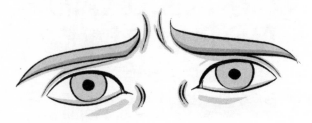

By **DaBesst99**.

AND ALL BECAUSE OUR IDIOT TEAMMATE DISTRACTED ME.

'It's okay,' Alfie tells me, 'I got your reboot card! I can... '

And then a shotgun goes CRACK and Alfie falls too.

You don't have to put up with people acting like **6DogTag8** did just now.

If someone is using abusive language over the voice or text chat, you can report them using the Report Player function on the menu.

You'll be given a list of reasons and can select a player you've played with or against recently.

You can also report players for:

OFFENSIVE SCREEN NAMES
I think you know what I mean by that!

HARASSMENT
For instance, if a player is targeting a particular player, seeking them out and messing up their game.

Fortnite helps protect you from this, because players don't see opponents' names until after they're eliminated, so it's hard for them to target a particular person. But if it's going on, you can report it.

SOLO TEAM-UPS

In Solo mode you're not meant to work with other players. This gives them an unfair advantage. If you see players teaming up, grab some video evidence and report them.

PLAYERS WHO JOIN A MATCH BUT DON'T PLAY

These guys are taking up space in the game - they'll get caught in the storm eventually, but in the meantime they're racking up XP just by participating which isn't really fair.

If you report a player they can be banned, so you may feel it's fair to give them a warning first.

And make sure that when you report a player, you have a good reason. If you report other players just to get them in trouble, you could be the one who ends up in trouble.

CHAPTER 9

So I'm walking to school, still cross about what happened yesterday.

Looking up I see I'm passing the supermarket, the fire station, the bank...

If this was Fortnite, which of those would be best to land on?

The supermarket will have food, but I don't need it if I've just landed and I'm at full health.

There may be more loot in the bank... but the fire station has a flat roof. Safer.

The sloping roof of the bank would leave me exposed - one shot with a sniper rifle could take me out.

I'll smash my way down through the fire station, grab all the loot, stand by an upper-floor window and take out anyone walking down the street.

On the pavement outside the fire station -

An ammo crate!

ACTUALLY A RECYCLING BOX

I search it, finding light ammo and shotgun cartridges, and move on.

Keeping in the cover of a low wall, I look up and see
the perfect getaway...

I get ready to hop onto it – when I hear footsteps approaching behind me! No time to build any cover – I just dive over the wall, crouch down and wait to ambush my opponent...

'Tyler? What are you doing?' says Sana.

It was her footsteps I heard. She was trying to catch up with me to say hi. And here I am, hiding in someone's front garden.

'Er... nothing,' I reply.

My head's so stuck in Fortnite, I'm seeing it everywhere.

I keep looking up at ceilings and wondering if I'd find a chest in the attic if I smashed through them.

When I look at walls and furniture I wonder what they'd drop if I harvested them: wood or brick?

When I check the map on my phone I expect to see a storm circle.

It's possible I'm a bit too obsessed with this game.

Then I hear another voice.

Typical. You find a good hiding place, and it turns out there's an NPC there.

I hop over the wall and Sana and I head for school.

I mumble something about what Leon said she said about me being useless.

'And you believed him?' she says.

I admit I did. But when she says it, I realise that was kind of stupid. Of course Leon would make out she agreed with him.

'I never said that,' she says.

I tell her I'm sorry, and how Leon's been winding me up for ages. I give her the full story of how he eliminated me yesterday.

'I've been playing loads and I can survive into the top ten or twenty almost every match now,' I say, 'but when I get to the endgame I mess it up and I'm never going to beat him.'

And then she says: 'Do you want some help?'

I don't just want help, I NEED help!

I should have admitted that earlier, really.

'OK,' she says, nodding. 'Come over to mine after school.'

I'm so grateful I say yes without really thinking about it. It's not until afterwards that I realise - **I've never been to her house before.**

NEW LOCATION! SANA'S HOUSE

PERFECT LANDING SPOT!

Sana's house is narrow but weirdly tall. (If you landed on the roof you could collect a lot of loot on the way down, I think.)

Her mum makes a big deal of me when we walk in, saying Sana never lets her meet her friends, and offers me various snacks.

But Sana is pulling on my arm. 'C'mon, let's get going,' she says.

'Thanks for the cakes,' I say.

'Okay Tyler,' Sana says loudly, 'We've got homework to do! Art project! Fun!' and she starts heading towards the stairs.

I follow her, balancing a plate of snacks up three flights of stairs to get to Sana's room at the very top. By the time we're there it feels like we're not even in the same house as her mum, who's working on a laptop in the dining room.

'Why did you tell your mum we're doing homework?' I say quietly. 'Doesn't she let you play computer games? Or is it just Fortnite - does she think it's too violent?'

Sana rolls her eyes. 'No - if she knew we were playing computer games she'd want to join in, and she gets really competitive.'

Sana moves a pile of books off a chair and invites me to sit down. It's a small room and there's a lot of stuff in it. She finds a laptop under a beanbag chair, turns it on and slumps on the beanbag. We start a Duos match together.

While we're waiting for it to load, she plugs a gaming headset into her laptop, then looks up at me while she puts them in her ears. 'Did you bring earphones?'

'I haven't got any earphones.'

Sana looks at me, surprised, and pulls her headphones down so they rest around her neck. 'You mean you don't use earphones when you play?'

'No, why?'

'You'll see,' she says.

Sana opens a drawer in her desk and rummages around in it. (I'm not trying to snoop, but I notice there's a purple wristband for the school disco in there.)

She finds a spare headset, untangles the cable, plugs it into my Switch and puts the thing on my head.

'This is my old one, I think it still works. OK?"

I mumble something that isn't yes and isn't no (yes because it's OK, no because it's a bit weird) and she goes back to her beanbag and we start the match.

Anyway, we start the match... and **WOW**.

It's totally different playing with earphones. Straight away I can find chests more easily - I can hear where the shimmery noise is coming from, so I know when there's one on the other side of a roof or in a sealed attic.

And even more useful than that, I can hear where gunfire's coming from, I can hear where footsteps are coming from. Suddenly I've got a much better idea what's going on.

This also makes me realise how easily other players can work out where I am, if they're using earphones too.

I knew stealth was important... but now I really get it.

Sound is a really useful tool in Fortnite. Everyone needs to listen out. So don't turn your microphone on and then make loads of noise!

I'm not just talking about people being abusive to other players here. If you keep chattering on about nothing, or talk to your friends or your parents, or you play in the same room as a sibling who's screaming at the top of their voice, you're ruining the game for everyone else in your squad.

So, whatever you do - DON'T SPAM THE CHAT.

Chat can be incredibly useful, but keep it for strategy discussions and warning teammates of danger. If you don't have a quiet place to play, turn it off!

So Sana and I move around the map as a team for a while, and we're in the last ten.

We take an opponent in a pincer movement. Sana distracts him with some quick running and noisy SMG fire - that's submachine gun - and he doesn't see (or hear) me crouch-walking in from the side.

A few quick shots with a pistol and he's toast.

He drops his loot, and it's awesome! There's an epic hunting rifle, a legendary burst assault rifle...

I run over, glancing down my inventory to work out what I need most -

And then I'm eliminated.

'When you get to the endgame,' says Sana, 'don't hang around in the open. Not for anything.'

It's obvious. Or it should have been. 'I got distracted by all the shiny shiny loot.'

Always take a moment to check your surroundings before you dive in and collect loot dropped by other players - not just in the endgame, but generally.

If you're the one who killed them, their teammate could be nearby, or other players may have heard the firefight.

They might be waiting to pick off the winner, who will probably be low on health, shields and maybe ammo too.

So don't think you can relax just because your immediate opponent has been dealt with!

Similarly, if you come across a load of dropped loot, it's possible the winner of this fight had a full inventory and couldn't carry all this stuff, or couldn't hang around... or it might be that the victim just got taken out by a sniper rifle before you got there, and the sniper could still be watching!

You can also use these tactics yourself, of course – if you see a firefight happening and the participants don't know you're there, you can take on the winner.

Or you can leave loot to tempt other players out of hiding, and watch over it with a sniper rifle.

'Sorry,' Sana says, 'I wish I could come over there to reboot you, but I don't think it's safe.'

She's right. Rebooting is easier early on in the match: players are more spread out, you're doing a lot of moving around anyway, and there are lots of reboot vans to choose from.

But during the endgame, it can be a risky business.

It involves a quick dash to pick up a reboot card, then a dash to whichever reboot vans are still in the storm circle. That's a lot of moving around, which is exactly what you want to avoid at this stage.

And then you'll be standing at the van for what feels like ages while you reboot your teammate.

You can help protect yourself when you reach the reboot van by throwing up some cover while you stand there.

Even better, put out a decoy or two - this is a great use for decoys.

If your decoys do get shot at while you're standing by the van, your opponents will have given away their positions - and when your teammate is ready to rejoin the action, you can work on a strategy to tackle them.

But it's good to reboot teammates if you can. I've played matches where I've rebooted a teammate, then died myself, and they've returned the favour by bringing me back.

I was genuinely quite touched.

You... came back for me!

'It's OK,' I tell Sana. 'Don't worry about rebooting me, I'll just leave the match.'

I might go downstairs and get some more snacks from her mum.

'No - stay and watch. You can learn loads by watching other players.'

This has never occurred to me before.

Usually when I get eliminated and there's no chance of getting rebooted, I just quit in a rage and start another match.

(Like when you've done something embarrassing and just want to get out of the room.)

I flip and watch one of the other surviving players - **Konkeror005**. I'm surprised to find that not only is she not inside the storm circle, she's miles away. She's out there in the storm, running around a building and opening chests.

What is she doing?

'Oh no!' says Sana, who's just run into a crowd of marauders while trying to reach a safe place, and has been eliminated.

That's her out now too, but she was close to a victory there, as there's only four players left, and one of them's wandering around in the storm like an idiot.

Sana switches to watch **Konkeror005** too.

'Her XP is really high, so she must have some idea what she's doing. Mustn't she?'

But both of us think it's totally weird.

She's got great weapons, including a legendary bolt-action sniper rifle (ooh!) and full shields. But shields don't protect you from the storm...

A new storm circle appears and finally **Konkeror005** stops messing about and heads towards it.

But she's got so far to go! How can she possibly get there? Her health drops to 12: she stops and heals, using one of the three medi kits she's just picked up.

Then she finds a zip wire and hops on it. I realise this one is long, and will take her near the storm circle.

She heals again along the way...

At the end of the zipwire she runs for the storm circle and heals the moment she's inside...

Konkeror005 is on top of a mountain and the only other remaining player is also running towards the storm circle, through a valley. She raises her sniper rifle, aims -

And takes him out. **VICTORY ROYALE!**

I can't believe what I've just seen, and there's no way I'd ever play like that - but Sana was right, it is interesting seeing how other people play.

You can pick up tips, and you can get an idea of what your opponents might be doing.

Plus, if you leave the match early, you're not going to share in the victory if your squad mates win!

With Sana's help, I get more experience of what the endgame's like.

It's weird how different it can be in different matches - lots of things can affect this - but one of the main factors is where the storm circle ends up.

If it's in an area with lots of buildings, there'll be places to hide. If this happens, find somewhere safe and be prepared to wait it out.

But if it closes around an area of open countryside, you'll have to build your own cover and watch out for other players, who might be coming from any direction.

Good players see this situation coming, and start building quickly.

The important thing is not to be running around in the open at this stage of the match.

Assume you're being watched all the time!

If you're on the move and hear gunfire, start throwing up walls!

If they're not shooting at you and you need to move on, you won't have lost anything... except the wood that you used for the walls.

By this stage you should have collected plenty of materials, just by searching chests and bashing your way through buildings.

You certainly don't want to be harvesting materials in the endgame – it makes noise and means you can't keep your gun drawn.

If you really have to, just take a couple of bashes at a structure and then stop before it collapses and draws attention to your positon.

A vanishing wall leaves you exposed to enemy fire, and a vanishing tree makes it really obvious where you are!

Another factor affecting the endgame is how many other players are left. The more there are, the more chaotic the endgame will be.

If you're up against two or three other players, you'll often find they're more patient and willing to wait for you to make a move.

(And if you're playing a Squads match, the number of teammates you have left will affect things.)

What's really annoying is that sometimes the storm circle closes around an area with NPCs in it.

It's better if you don't have to deal with NPCs at this stage of the game - the other players are more important. And getting into combat with NPCs will give away your position to other players.

On the other hand, when you take down an NPC they sometimes drop awesome weapons, which might make all the difference when it gets to the final moments of the match. And the endgame is when your stock of weapons really come into play.

Destroying your opponent's fort is much easier with a rocket launcher!

The problem is, you don't know what sort of weapons will be best suited to the endgame until you get there, so how do you know what to bring?

If the endgame happens in a built-up area, you need good short-range weapons: shotguns, pistols and SMGs. Explosives are less useful, unless you get a chance to trap an opponent in a room.

An endgame in an open area needs medium and long-range weapons. After you've built your fort, a sniper rifle is ideal.

Explosives and anything that's good for destroying structures will help you strike at your opponent's fort.

Decoys are especially useful in the open, because they're more likely to be seen.

This is why it's important to watch as the storm circle shrinks, and try to get an idea of how things are going to play out.

Sometimes you're just running towards it to keep safe – but if you can, take a moment to look at what area it's shrinking around.

A lot of your choices about what weapons to take and what to drop will be driven by what you happen to find - if you come across a legendary hunting rifle you'll want to keep it, whatever the endgame's going to be like.

And it also depends what weapons you're good at using.

But often, as you're heading for a shrinking storm circle, you'll come across a weapon that's a different type, but a similar class, to what you're already carrying, and you'll have to choose whether to drop something and take that instead.

Think about how the endgame is shaping up, and that might help your decision.

The same goes for when you eliminate other players during the endgame. When their loot spills out, grab what's useful to you now - don't just grab stuff because it looks cool.

If you feel like you've already got the right weapons for the situation, only take theirs if it's an upgrade on what you've got.

While you're hiding, always plan your escape route. In fact, come up with more than one escape route, because your first choice may be closed off.

If you're hiding in a building, know how you're going to get out if the storm circle moves and you're no longer in it.

If the circle cuts you off, or if a bunch of NPCs come through the building, you may need to bash down a wall or the floor to get out, so plan which one.

And make sure you know what you'll be walking into when you leave the building - will there be cover?

Are you likely to run into other players?

If you're taking cover in your own fort, make sure you know where you're going to go next, if you need to leave it behind.

Know which weapon you'll need when you're on the move, and have it ready!

You can also use hiding time to reload all your weapons.

But be aware that switching between different weapons makes noise, and so you may attract the attention of other players.

If you're sure there's no-one around - or if you're confident of shooting them first if they burst in on your hiding place - then having fully loaded weapons can make all the difference in a firefight.

By the end of my session with Sana, I've added another Victory Royale to my stats – but again I didn't survive to see the end of it. I got eliminated by another duo who teamed up on me.

So it still doesn't really feel like it counts.

'Does all that help?' says Sana, taking off her earphones.

'Yeah, it's great,' I tell her, putting the headset back in the drawer (and seeing the purple wristband again). 'Still not sure how I'm going to tackle Leon though.'

Sana thinks. 'He doesn't do much building – he lets teammates do it. He's good with long-range weapons and he's got quick reactions. But even if you get put in a match together again, there's not much chance of you coming up against him, so don't worry about it.'

'I do worry about it, though,' I say. 'I don't want him getting me again and then lording it over me – I just want to get him back. I HAVE to get him back, and I'm still not good enough yet.'

Sana leans back in the beanbag chair. 'It sort of feels like you're forgetting to have fun, Tyler.'

'I'm not, I just -' I start to say. Then I realise she's right.

I have forgotten to have fun.

'Speaking of fun,' she says, 'are you going to the disco?'

I shrug. 'I don't really dance.'

'That's a shame,' she says. 'Anyway we need to make up an art project we can pretend we've been working on in case my mum asks – you got any ideas?'

CHAPTER 10

So I've taken Sana's advice. I've stopped worrying about Leon and what he's doing.

Now I'm just focusing on my own game.

'Oh good,' says Alfie when I tell him this, and he looks properly pleased about it.

I think he was getting a bit weirded out by how obsessed I was with killing one of my best friends in a computer game.

Which is fair enough.

Sana has managed to get Ellie to join us for a Squads match, having convinced her I've got a lot better at the game and won't drag the team down.

We, er, haven't told her who's going to be filling the fourth spot...

'Who is that?' says Ellie over the chat.

That's Alfie,' Sana says over the chat – neither Alfie
nor I have a microphone so she's doing the talking for
all of us. 'He's Tyler's mate.'

'Is he any good?' says Ellie.

There's a silence. Alfie looks over at Sana with an innocent expression on his face, waiting to hear what she's going to say.

He only met Sana an hour ago, and he explained his no-killing policy to her. She nodded slowly and said 'Okay...'

Then she watched while he and I played a Duos match, because I thought it was important for her to understand that he really does play like that.

Ellie doesn't sound convinced, but we're in the lobby now, so whatever, we're playing.

Straight away it's clear Ellie isn't interested in following the same strategy as the rest of us.

She bails out of the Battle Bus over the centre of the map, while the rest of us go to the edge, taking different buildings in the same cluster and grabbing loot.

I keep an eye on the updates at the edge of the screen. Ellie's survived the early skirmishes, and has notched up five kills in a couple of minutes. (She uses the voice chat to keep us updated on her total.)

Sana tells her she's distracting us all.

'You're just jealous,' mutters Ellie.

Meanwhile, we're in a beach hut and Alfie's found a flare gun. 'Do you want this or shall I carry it?' he says.

'You carry it,' I say.

'OK,' says Alfie.

Next thing I know, the beach hut is on fire.

'What happened?!' Sana and I both shout.

'I think I fired the flare gun by mistake,' says Alfie.
'Yep, that's definitely what's happened.'

We bail out of the hut. Alfie and I have both taken serious damage – his health is down to 9 – but we're still in the match.

Which, it turns out, is more than you can say for Ellie.

She's got into one firefight too many and she was observing Alfie when he had his flare gun mishap.

'That's the dumbest thing I've ever seen,' she says over the chat.

'Don't neg your teammates, Ellie,' says Sana while she throws Chug Splash over Alfie and me.

**But it's true, this isn't a promising start.
We've lost Ellie and we've set fire to ourselves.**

'You guys head for the storm circle,' says Alfie, as if he's in charge.

Before I can ask him what he's doing, he's got in a car and driven off.

Sana and I start running. We've got a long way to go.

'Sorry!' says Alfie at one point.

'What for?' I ask.

'Oh not you - I was talking to this guy I just ran over.'

'Is one of you using a car?' says Ellie suspiciously: she's spectating Sana's game. 'I don't like cars, they're too noisy.'

'You don't like any vehicles,' says Sana.

A few moments later, Alfie has picked up Ellie's reboot card, driven to a reboot van, brought her back into the match and given her an assault rifle and grenades!

She reluctantly admits cars might not be that bad after all...

...and maybe you're not that dumb, Alfie.

The four of us head for the storm circle. It's already getting close to the endgame...

Building can be your best weapon. Watch the best players and you'll see they do a lot of building.

When it gets to the endgame, scope out where you've ended up. Grab the highest ground, unless it's already been taken - and then build quickly! There usually isn't much cover on the higher ground, and other players will probably be able to see you up there.

A fort on a hill is the strongest position to defend. (Just ask all those mediaeval guys who built castles.)

It's true.

Our endgame is in a terrible place - a flat plane of land, with very little cover and a river running through the middle. So there is no higher ground to find. Sana and I take cover behind a car (there's no way we're driving it - we don't want to give away our position).

We've got our backs to the storm...

Then someone runs at us out of the storm, guns blazing. I shoot back and miss - but Sana quickly builds two flights of stairs with a platform at the top. I run up there and shoot down at our attacker. It only takes one shot with a pistol to take him out.

Got him! A one-shot kill!

Hmmm. He probably took a lot of damage in the storm.

'Yeah but I still got him. Let me have some credit.'

More shots come from inside the storm circle - we've attracted attention. But I throw up more walls and stairs while Sana eliminates the player who's rushing at us.

We agree this can't be our final fort as it's going to be swallowed by the storm in a minute, so we head towards Alfie and Ellie...

Building two or three flights of stairs and then putting a platform at the top is a good move to practise. This is where keyboard users have the advantage - if you bind keys to certain structures, you can build with a few quick key-presses.

Sana has her laptop and her hand flashes across the keys.

TAP TAP TAPATAPA TAP TAPTAP

This is a really useful trick if you find yourself battling another player in the open and want to quickly get some cover and a height advantage.

It'll usually take your opponent by surprise and you can get a shot or two in before they can build some cover for themselves - but be quick!

This technique can also be used to get around an opponent's defences. Lots of players don't bother building a roof on their fort, and you can surprise them by building stairs that give you a view over the top of it, then firing down at them.

This works best if you can do it without them noticing, so look for cover while you build, and work fast!

Don't dither around trying to make your stairway connect up. And of course, build a roof on your own forts and stop other players doing this to you!

In our match, I don't need to make a fort. Alfie's already made a pretty good one.

'Wow,' says Sana.

'He kept stopping to pick up materials,' Ellie grumbles. 'But fair enough, it is a decent fort.'

We agree to each watch different directions – I stand at the back and check if anyone else is coming out of the storm, Ellie and Sana stand at either side of the fort and look out for any movement at the front. Alfie's ready to repair our fort in case anyone attacks.

Suddenly it's all gone very quiet. There's a couple of small forts out there, but it looks like whoever was in them, they've been eliminated.

Then Sana says: 'Someone's building another fort over there. Trying to make it bigger than ours.'

As I said before, when it comes to building, height is more important than width – so if you're in a hurry, build upwards.

But if the match develops into a sniper battle, where you and one or two other players are sitting in your forts trying to get a glimpse of each other, that's the one time a wide fort can be useful. Your opponent will find it harder to guess where you're going to shoot from next, and it'll take them longer to find their aim when you do pop up to take a shot at them.

Staying behind cover, add more walls to your fort and put stairs behind. You can also add some windows to give yourself more shooting positions, but be careful not to stand at them too long!

Ellie loves using the sniper rifle, so she looses off a few shots, ducking back behind cover each time - but she can't get a good shot. The enemy is staying under cover. But Ellie thinks they're within assault rifle range, so she fires at a wall, breaks it down -

And it appears again. They've just built it straight back up.

Ellie keeps firing and breaks it down again -

And they build it again.

'They're spamming walls,' says Sana.

'I can see that,' says Ellie.

'Stop it! You're going to run out of ammo!'

'Maybe they'll run out of materials first...'

They don't run out of materials first, and soon Ellie's assault rifle is empty.

There's seven players left in the match and Sana's pretty sure all the others are a squad – which means we'll all be needed if we're going to win...

If the other players left in the match are teammates that will affect your strategy.

For instance, it's no good hoping they might eliminate each other. Watch their behaviour and see if you can work it out!

When you get into a stalemate situation, with both sets of players hiding in their forts, it often comes down to luck: the storm circle shrinks and one of you is forced to move while the other one can stay put...

Sure enough, the storm circle moves and we're not inside it.

'We're gonna have to move,' says Sana. 'We've only got a minute before it closes in.'

Alfie doesn't seem to want to move.

'Nooo... we can't abandon my beautiful fort...'

But then I remember something. 'Alfie - have you still got that flare gun? The one you set fire to the beach hut with?'

'Yeah.'

'Why didn't you say sooner?'

'I assumed you knew. I mean, I did set fire to you with it.'

I tell Alfie to give the flare gun to Ellie. She wants to get closer, and hit as many parts of the fort as possible. Sana and I will give her covering fire...

Ellie hits the fort once, twice, three times - it starts to burn...

But she takes a headshot from a rifle. She's gone!

No way back for her this time - but Sana gets a clear shot at the sniper and takes them down.

Five players left...

One of the opposing squad runs from the burning fort, shooting at us and hitting Alfie. We shoot back - he's taken damage from the fire so goes down easily.

But the other player LAUNCHES himself out of the fort (he must have a launch pad)...

And lands in the remains of someone else's abandoned fort and starts rebuilding!

It's three against one. Our opponent's managed to find a new fort - and we have to move out of ours like, now. The storm's moving.

And also, one of us is a pacifist and won't use weapons.

'What do we do?' says Alfie.

He sounds weirdly calm. I guess you can be calm when you're not that bothered about winning.

I realise the fort our opponent has moved to isn't as tall as ours. And it's not that far away.

'Have you got decoys?' I ask Alfie.

'Yeah.'

'How many?'

'Nine.'

'Nine?!' says Sana.

'I gave all my guns to Ellie. And I like decoys.'

'So, we need you to create the biggest diversion ever,' I tell Alfie...

Sana and I head for the top of Alfie's fort. By the time we get there, Alfie is already running across the ground between our fort and theirs.

He throws down decoy after decoy, and pretty soon we're looking down at ten Alfies running around!

Sana starts building a platform connecting our fort with the other one and I run across it, being careful not to run off the end...

In moments we're looking down into the fort. Our opponent is completely distracted by the army of Alfies marching towards him! I raise my shotgun and shoot once, twice, three times -

AND THAT'S VICTORY ROYALE.

Standing on the platform, Sana and I do a victory dance. It's the greatest feeling. Better than ice cream on your birthday. Even Ellie's cheering.

And then I get a message notification.

YOU HAVE A FRIEND REQUEST FROM: DABESST99

And I get a text:

> Yeah, OK. Good shot mate. I'll get you next time.

Was that... Leon??

This is better than ten ice creams on your birthday.

CHAPTER 11

The following evening Sana and I are hanging around outside the school together, waiting for it to open and the disco to start.

'You played any Fortnite since your epic victory yesterday?' she says.

'*Our* epic victory,' I say. 'And no, I'm taking a day off.'

'Wow. When I win a match I always want to play another one straight away because I think I'm awesome! I want to win again!'

'Me too. But when I lose, I also want to play again straight away because I want to make up for whatever mistake got me killed last time.'

Sana smiles. 'Me too.'

'So... did you know Leon and Jake would be in that match?'

(Jake, it turns out, was the one who got elimated at the very end, when he ran out of the burning fort.)

'Seems like a bit of a coincidence.'

Sana smiles and admits she might have texted Leon to let them know when we started our match.

(Of course, you can't guarantee you'll end up in the same match if you're not playing on the same squad – but if you go into the lobby at the same time, you often do.)

But because I didn't know he was there, I wasn't thinking about proving anything to him.

I was just thinking about winning the match.

'So, you tricked me,' I say.

She shrugs. 'Little bit. But it worked, didn't it?'

'So I've had a couple of offers to join a squad,' I say casually.

Sana raises an eyebrow. 'From who?'

'Well, you missed all the fun at lunchtime today, didn't you?'

Sana was at her drama group, so Ellie and I just watched as Jake completely lost it with Leon for bouncing away to that other fort rather than helping him fight us in the open.

'Jake shouted

"YOU HUNG ME OUT TO DRY!"

and stormed off,' I tell Sana. 'Says he'll never play with Leon again.'

Sana laughs. 'He's said that before. They'll make it up.'

'Probably. But in the meantime, Leon's asked me if I can replace Jake on the squad, and Jake's asked me if I can replace Leon. Somehow Leon thinks Jake has quit and Jake thinks he's thrown Leon out.'

'Don't Ellie and me get a say in all this?'

'Ellie wants to replace them both with Alfie. She thinks he's ace. She really likes having someone to do all the building and rebooting and decoy runs while she can just focus on shooting people.'

Sana laughs again. Making her laugh is almost as good as when I beat Leon.

The school doors open up and we're allowed in. Just inside, Maisie's standing there with her tray of wristbands. I wonder if she's going to actually go to her own disco or if she's going to spend the whole time selling these.

She points at our purple wristbands. 'Can I interest you in an upgrade? Orange gets you access to the VIP –'

'I'm OK thanks,' says Sana.

I fumble in my pocket for some coins. 'Actually, I'll pay for us both to have one, if I've got enough.'

Sana turns to me. 'What if you haven't got enough?'

'Well, then I'll just pay for you.'

Luckily I do have enough.

And it turns out dancing is my thing.

I mean, I'm not very good at it. But I like it.

COMING SOON...

SECRETS OF A FORTNITE FAN - LAST SQUAD STANDING

Tyler Meeks is no longer a complete Fortnite
noob - but he's still got a lot to learn. And the
world of Fortnite keeps changing...
Has Tyler got what it takes
to lead his own squad?

Join Tyler, Alfie and their friends as they learn
how to work together in this all new Fortnite
adventure, packed with tactics, tricks and
secrets to help you make your team the
LAST SQUAD STANDING!

Yes, it's true, Tyler Meeks has

NEVER PLAYED FORTNITE!

But with the help of his friends, that's about to change...

Follow Tyler's hilarious quest for his first Victory Royale! This laugh-out-loud story is filled with awesome illustrations, plus REAL GAMEPLAY TIPS, TRICKS and SECRETS. So YOU can become an ultimate Fortnite master too!

www.welbeckpublishing.com

ISBN: 978-1-83935-045-0

£5.99
Children's

9 781839 350450

9266.01 Printed in the UK